High Jinks in Hedingham is a collection of light-hearted children's poems and stories inspired by historical events in the village of Castle Hedingham where the Norman invader, Aubrey de Vere, built a castle that would become the ancestral home of the Earls of Oxford.

With a brief nod to actual fact; a lot of silly nonsense; and vibrant illustrations, the stories transport the modern-day reader back to events as they may (or may not!) have occurred in the village of Castle Hedingham during the reign of the House of Normandy.

HIGH JINKS IN HEDINGHAM

Written and illustrated by Carol Sullivan Johnson.

© 2022. All rights reserved.

CONTENTS

AUBREY BUILDS A CASTLE 6

YOUNG AUBREY'S ADVENTURES 19

THE KING'S DINNER 30

THE TALE OF TWO MATILDAS 46

THE SIEGE OF HEDINGHAM CASTLE 55

THE EARL'S NEW SHOES 71

AUBREY BUILDS A CASTLE

A Norman knight and his wife

Young Aubrey was a knight

Who loved a good fight.

And William, his mate, had ambition.

"I reckon," Will bragged,

"I could rouse up a gang

And take England - my rightful possession."

"Cause this here's the thing -

I should be the new king,

But that Harold's taken the call.

I've just as much right,

So I'm up for the fight.

Come join me - winner takes all."

Well, that sounded good

And Aubrey stood

To gain a great deal from the venture,

So he informed the wife -

Which caused him some strife -

Then he ran off with William the Conqueror.

With their cunning plan hatched

And Harold dispatched

By a lucky shot (right in the face!),

Saxon rule fell,

The kingdom was Will's,

And the Normans now reigned in their place.

A lucky shot (right in the face!)

Now, pinching a kingdom

Is not for the faint,

The fickle, or weary of heart,

And William could tell

For this to end well,

He'd have to be smart from the start.

So he sent out his men

Again and again

To record everything that they found,

So he knew who was what

And what they'd all got,

From the cows to the oats in the ground.

And as a reward

For their loyalty sworn,

He gave his barons some land.

Booting out Saxon lords,

By the edge of their swords,

They built posh new homes, great and grand.

So Aubrey went east

To establish his seat

('Cause King Will gave him a charter)

Right on the top of a ridge

Where the wife and the kids

Could live happily forever after.

High up on a spur

The location preferred -

He could see miles in every direction.

He'd soon throw up a mound

With a moat all around

And a bridge with a gate for protection.

Well, if Aubrey could see

How it was to be

When his wife got wind of the deal!

The argument raged

All night and all day -

"You expect us to live up that great hill?"

She wasn't impressed.

She became quite distressed.

"It's hardly a palace, now, is it?

When my friends come to tea,

You'll embarrass me

And *NOBODY* will want to visit!"

"It's rocky and bare!

We'll grow nothing there

And the wind will blow us away!

I want somewhere cosy

With hollyhocks and roses,

And shade from the heat of the day."

"But babe," Aubrey countered,

"There's so much advantage

To living on top of a crest.

You can pull up a pew

In a room with a view

To the north, south, the east or the west."

"Well, what good is the view

From a window or two,

When all you can see are some trees?"

Came the wailing reply,

With a sniff, and the sigh

Of a wife who wasn't too pleased.

So the decision was made

And Aubrey just prayed

It would turn out okay in the end,

'Cause what he proposed

Was more than a home -

It was a whacking great fortress, my friend.

The first thing to do…

Clear a tree or two,

Then start hacking away at the rock

'Til a huge ditch appeared

And a big earth mound reared

Up from the soil piled on top.

It was a whacking great fortress, my friend!

Then up went the wall

Surrounding it all…

("A *MASSIVE* one!" Aubrey would gloat)

Made of timber, all spiked -

The way Aubrey liked -

With a rickety bridge over the moat.

Next came the house,

Raised up, off the ground,

Sort of like where you keep chickens.

And then, underneath,

For the goats and the sheep,

Some pens with sides made of wicker.

"This just won't do!"

Yelled his wife, in a stew.

"I only came 'cause you said I oughta.

We left lovely grounds

With gardens around,

And a moat that actually had *WATER!*"

Now, Aubrey knew

What he had to do

To stop his wife giving him hassle,

So he promised one day,

It would be swept away,

And replaced with a mighty stone castle.

And there it sits now -

The thumping, great tower

Thrown up on the very same hill,

Where the first Aubrey stood,

In his fort made of wood,

In the land he'd invaded with Will.

And there it sits now - the thumping great tower

And now the true story...

Before he became the King of England, William the Conqueror was the powerful Duke of Normandy. Along with other powerful rulers and blood relatives, he had been promised the English throne by the childless king, Edward the Confessor. However, upon his deathbed, Edward seemed to accept Harold Godwinson, the mighty Earl of Wessex, as his successor.

In 1066, William the Conqueror landed his troops at Pevensey, in East Sussex, and fought a pitched battle against Harold. Harold was struck in the face by an arrow and died, leaving William to declare his victory over the Anglo-Saxon people and become the first in a succession of Norman kings.

The Normans took land from the existing Anglo-Saxon lords and introduced sweeping changes to the way their English subjects were now to live. The invading Normans spoke French, which then became the language of the nobility, while the lower classes still spoke an old form of English. Ruthless in his battle to suppress the English people, particularly in the north, William brutally put down any form of opposition by existing Anglo-Saxon lords.

In the first years of his reign, William sent out inspectors to every part of his new kingdom to record the population and assets of every town and village. This book, which has two volumes and is housed in the British Library, is called the 'Domesday Book'. It is estimated that the population of England at the time may have been about two million people. Both Great and Little Yeldham, villages nearby Castle Hedingham, are listed in the Domesday Book.

Along with other estates in Suffolk and Cambridgeshire, the estate of Hedingham was awarded to Aubrey de Vere I by 1086, a motte and bailey castle being built on top of a domineering rocky outcrop in the years following. His son, Aubrey II, began building the keep and Aubrey de Vere III completed it in about 1140. By 1180, work had begun on the church of St Nicholas, around which the ancient village of Castle Hedingham would eventually establish itself.

Aubrey III, by this time the Earl of Oxford, also founded a Benedictine priory at the foot of the castle mound sometime around 1190. This was to be a nunnery – exclusively for the use of women. It survived until its dissolution during the reign of Henry VIII. It was not, apparently, a welcome addition to their growing community as far as some of the men involved with the de Vere family were concerned. The Earl's son, Aubrey IV, had his men set it to the torch!

Later on, in the 13th century, a hospital was also founded at the foot of the castle mound. This caused the nuns of the priory some consternation, as they considered tending the sick and poor to be their line of business. Of course, their concern was not only about their philanthropic endeavours – they saw the hospital's existence as a threat to their income source.

Hospitals in those days were not like those we may be familiar with today. Two or three chaplains were invested there to say daily prayers for Hugh de Vere, the fourth Earl of Oxford, and his wife, so it was very much a private chapel for the de Veres. Income donated to the hospital for the relief of the poor would be effectively diverted from the priory coffers. Eventually, an agreement was made that the hospital would pay the priory one-tenth of its income (called a 'tithe') and everybody was happy.

YOUNG AUBREY'S ADVENTURES

A row of tumbledown cottages in the village below

Scorching rays from an unusually fierce summer sun beat down mercilessly on the parched ground of the upper bailey of Hedingham Castle. The earth was cracked and bare, and every last wisp of green grass had withered into crisp, brown chaff. Not a breath of air moved to offer relief from the stifling heat that rose in shimmering waves up the sides of the rocky outcrop on which the castle had been raised.

All activity had ceased as the occupants of the castle had taken themselves indoors to escape the sultry heat of the noonday sun. Only the long, lazy cawing of crows broke the breathless silence. Their plaintive cries drifted monotonously upwards from somewhere beyond the open fields bordering the village that lay at the foot of the castle's steep hill.

Suddenly, a young boy, about five years of age, appeared from behind a range of buildings that ran along the inside of the castle's stone curtain wall. With a furtive, backward glance, he made his way over to the outer wall and crept along its smooth face, keeping close and low, as if to avoid detection. Stopping at the base of a set of steps that gave access to the top of the wall, the young child turned his head to look from side to side, then cautiously began to climb the stairs. Soon, his small, bare head peeped over the top of the wall and the vast expanse of the countryside beyond spread out before him.

Young Aubrey craned his neck to see as far as he could. A rutted, winding track curved down the slope of the hill from the lower bailey of the castle. It forked at the bottom, bleeding into the well-trampled, bare earth between the ranges of brick buildings at the base of the hill. Here Aubrey could often catch glimpses of the spectre-like Benedictine nuns in their formless black habits as they went about their daily routine - tending the sick and the poor peasants of the village; tending the gardens that grew their food;

and trekking back and forth to the solid, square-towered church (dedicated to St Nicholas) several times a day to tend to their own souls. The other fork in the rutted, dirt track emerged from the nun's complex and wound its way past a row of tumbledown cottages made with mud and straw walls, and heavy, low thatched roofs.

Many months ago, Aubrey had stood and held his nurse's hand as he watched as his father and his attendants make their way on horseback along the same paths as they passed through the village. Clearing the ramshackle complex of buildings, and without a backward glance, the horse-mounted party had cantered briskly out of view. Aubrey's father's frame was straight and tall in the saddle of his favourite mare, both decked with the colours of the de Vere crest – yellow and red, with a five-pointed star. The great pride Aubrey had felt swelling up inside his chest as he watched his father's departure was tinged with sadness, as Aubrey knew that it may be a very long time before he would see him again.

Aubrey's father was rarely home. Of necessity, he spent long periods in the King's service, as well as dealing with the responsibilities of his various other estates. Travel was slow and difficult in those days, with roads that were little more than muddy cart tracks. News was sent by horseback, in letters sealed with a blob of melted, red wax into which the writer's sign had been pressed with a special stamp. The recipient of the letter would know it had not been opened or read by anyone else if it arrived with the seal still intact. Aubrey had never received such a letter.

From the castle wall, Aubrey could see far beyond the village to vast swathes of dense woodland that stretched out to the horizon. The uniform blanket of green was broken by strips of brown tilled earth where villagers grew grain and vegetables for the lord of the manor, his father. Rising from one spot or another in the forest were tell-tale wisps of smoke from woodmen's cottages hidden away in its deep, mysterious shadows.

The wood was a very dangerous place for a child as young as Aubrey, but his father and his friends delighted in spending their leisure hours there, hunting on horseback for wild boar and deer. Soon, Aubrey would be old enough to accompany the men as they went hunting and would grow strong enough to ride and shoot game for himself. But for now, he must be content to wait at the tall gate towers until he heard the excited noises of dogs, horses and men returning in triumph with their hard-won dinner.

On very rare excursions from his castle home, Aubrey had seen other children about his age, bare-legged and brown-skinned from the summer sun, splashing about in the shallow water at the ford in the river that ran past their village. How he had wished in those moments that he could leap from the cart on which he was travelling, throw off his leather shoes and leggings, and join in the fun! Although he was aware that he was born into a powerful and privileged family, he could not help but envy the children of his father's tenants who, unburdened by the restraints of lessons conducted by humourless tutors and a nurse who scrutinised every aspect of her charge's conduct, were free to run and play from dawn to dusk with neither boundary nor interference. Or so it seemed to him...

Our young boy's full name was Aubrey de Vere III, his father being Aubrey II, and his grandfather, Aubrey I. He had been born into a powerful noble family who served the kings of the House of Normandy – the conquerors of the Anglo-Saxons. Aubrey had been born at Hedingham Castle, which had been built high on a rocky outcrop in eastern England. It dominated gently rolling, productive land that stretched away in every direction, as far as the eye could see.

The castle that Aubrey's grandfather had built on the site had been typical of those raised by the Norman invaders. It had been a motte and bailey: an area enclosed by a curtain wall of wooden spikes (the bailey) inside which a large mound (the motte) was raised where the lord would build his residence. It was all surrounded by a moat for added defence. In the case of Hedingham Castle, a second bailey had been cleared and fenced on the outer edge of the dry, rock-hewn moat. Here, the livestock was housed and various household activities were performed, such as brewing, butchering, and metalworking. Over the years, the wooden fortifications and buildings had been replaced with stone and brick.

Being still a young child, the walls and gates of the castle were the boundaries of Aubrey's world – and it could be a somewhat dangerous world at that. It could also be a very lonely world for a small child, despite the ceaseless daily activity that was necessary to keep the castle functioning.

Each day, even before the cockerel crowed, the castle's army of servants rose to begin their day's toil. There was always work to do. The days seemed long and the work was hard and relentless. Copious amounts of water had to be fetched by lowering a bucket down to the bottom of the well via a rope, then heaving it back up again with its precious load. It was needed to keep the brewer supplied so he could ensure there was enough ale to drink. Nobody dared to drink plain water!

There was wood to be chopped and carted to the many firesides around the castle and the great ovens in the kitchens needed to be fed first (well before dawn) to begin the daily making of bread for the lord's breakfast. Then everyone else could be fed too.

The fires in the kitchen ovens were never permitted to quite die away. By early morning, the ashes in the kitchen fireplace would be glowing red and crackling behind its blackened metal grate. The smell of stale smoke and charred flesh still hung in the air. Flurries of ash and golden sparks would fly up into the air as the kitchen boys tossed a new batch of split logs into the slumbering embers. With renewed fierceness, orange and yellow flames would leap back to life and blaze away furiously.

Young kitchen hands, not much older than Aubrey himself, would turn the handle of a great spit on which the carcasses of whole animals were skewered for roasting. The kitchen fire burned with such intense heat that the boys who were given this unenviable task would often find that their own faces and hands were all but roasted as well!

In addition to the roasting spit, huge, blackened metal pots in which to make soups and stews were suspended by thick chains from the chimney breast. They hung above the fire embers all day, their contents slowly simmering away: chunks of the toughest of the butchered meats that came across the cook's long, scrubbed wood bench, with grains added for thickening the gravy. There was also a large bread oven on one side of the oven in which to bake the huge quantities of bread that were needed each day. Whether rich or poor, most people would eat several loaves of heavy wheat, rye or barley bread each and every day! Being wealthy, Aubrey's family ate meat every day as well as bread – particularly pork, chicken, and a delicacy that had been introduced from Normandy: rabbit. They also enjoyed beef and mutton, as well as goats, various types of birds, fish, and, of course, any wild animals that they hunted on their land. Aubrey was blissfully unaware of the meagre offerings in the homes of the poor farmworkers who barely carved out their living in the fields surrounding the castle. They usually ate something called 'pottage', which was a thick vegetable soup, or stew, based on boiled grains, such as oats or barley.

A solitary child, Aubrey had once sought out the company of the grimy-faced kitchen boys, hoping to find himself a playmate. Instead, he found himself being escorted unceremoniously out of the kitchen by the cook and returned to the care of his nurse. Poor Nurse had momentarily lost sight of him and been frantically searching for him in all the outbuildings of the upper bailey. "The kitchen," scolded Cook, "was no place for the child of the lord of the manor!"

It was not the first time Aubrey had fallen foul of the cook. Once, he had been given a wooden sword by his father and shown how to execute the best battle moves with it. It was the very beginning of training for warfare, so necessary for boys born into his position in life. With great enthusiasm, he ran across the inner compound, cutting and thrusting into the air with his wooden sword, practising being the best and bravest knight there ever was. "What would be really good," he reasoned to himself one day, "would be if I had an enemy to fight!"

The most obvious candidates for 'the enemy' were the many chickens that scuttled around the castle grounds, scratching in the dirt for bugs and squabbling over grain that fell from the daily kitchen deliveries. Aubrey would chase them around, darting and diving, trying to pre-empt where they would shoot off to next, swinging his sword wildly in their general direction. This seemed to Aubrey to be a wonderfully effective way of honing his sword-fighting skills. The cook didn't quite agree. Cook said it frightened the birds so much that they would stop laying their eggs. And the only good use there was for a chicken that had stopped laying eggs was to be put in the dinner pot!

Entertaining as it was to watch the birds being dispatched for the pot by chopping off their heads with an enormous, razor-sharp cleaver, apparently, this was too dangerous an activity in which Aubrey could be involved. He had so wanted to chase after the bodies of the headless chickens as they ran across the slaughter yard before they realised they were supposed to be dead! So, sadly, scaring the chickens joined a long list of things Aubrey was not supposed to do, along with hanging about in the lower bailey where the butcher in the slaughter yard went about his work.

Back at the high stone wall of the upper bailey, Aubrey lay his arms flat, elbows splayed outward along the hot, smooth blocks and rested his chin on the top of his downturned palms. He could feel the heat of the sun-baked stones burning through the linen of his tunic sleeves and, for as long as he could bear it, he pretended not to notice. Finally, he pulled back his arms and rubbed them vigorously in an attempt to deaden the pain.

It was no use. As much as he wanted to stay and search for movement in the landscape, the heat of the stone wall and the burning of the sun's rays on his uncovered head made him step back down into a sliver of shade on the stairs. At that moment, the anxious voice of his nurse called to him from the other side of the castle enclosure.

"Young master! Young master! Come down from the wall!" came the anxious cry of a woman who felt only too well the burden of responsibility for the young and mischievous (but extremely precious) child over whom she had been given charge. "Please come down. You may fall!"

Falling from the castle wall, although it had not been Aubrey's intention, may easily have become Aubrey's fate. The curtain wall surrounded the top of the hill on which the castle had been built and was designed as a defensive measure. It was thick and tall, wide enough at the top for an adult to walk along, with a precipitous drop on the outer edge that fell away down a steep slope and into the rocky, dry moat. A fall from such a great height would definitely have caused serious injury, such as broken bones, which, in the days before antibiotics, often led to death.

On more than one occasion, Nurse had found an adventurous Aubrey walking along the top of it, arms held out on both sides to maintain balance, as she stood below, begging him to come down. It was particularly challenging, and the most fun, when there was a high wind blowing; since Aubrey was never quite sure whether he could stay on his feet in the strongest gusts. Well, so far, so good! Unfortunately for Aubrey, and his nurse, many such dangers seemed to lurk around every corner of their castle home.

Aubrey's father was in the process of building a new keep, which is a tall, square tower with thick stone walls, which could be defended easily against attackers. The stone was quarried further afield and transported to the top bailey, ready for construction. Building sites and all their equipment were as fascinating for children then as they are now, and just as dangerous. Although Aubrey would have loved to watch the workmen at their labour and interrogate them about their activities (maybe even help), he was strictly forbidden to go anywhere near them or their project.

Another place Aubrey would have loved to play was on the bridge over the moat. It was a long, narrow, stone bridge with low walls on either side to stop people, as well as animals and carts of goods, from falling over the side and into the ditch below. Open at one end, it passed through a gatehouse on the curtain wall at the other end, with two towers on either side holding a spiked metal portcullis. A portcullis is a huge iron grill that would be lowered at night and in times of danger to prevent unwelcome visitors from entering the castle's inner compound.

Aubrey could think of a thousand games he would have loved to play on that bridge! He could drop stones over the edge and count how many seconds passed until they hit the bottom. He could see how far down the moat he could throw sticks, or whether his mother's fine linen handkerchiefs would float away on an updraft if he dropped them over the side. He could stand in the middle of the bridge and refuse to allow the peasants with their daily delivery of household goods to cross over. They would never dare to challenge the son of their lord! Aubrey could only imagine what a great game it would be to hide in the side tower of the gate and jump out to spook horses as they passed through it. Although there always remained a nagging temptation to try it, in his heart of hearts, Aubrey knew that doing such a thing would only result in outraged parents and severe punishment.

And then there was the well. How much fun it was to drop gravel into the well and listen for the 'plop, plop, plop' echoing back up from the watery depths below. "But," insisted Nurse, "if you fall into the well, we won't be able to get you out again!" So Aubrey was not permitted to drop things into the well. He was not even allowed to tie things onto the end of a long piece of rope and lower them into the well to see how far they went before they got wet. He had tried that once with a dead rat he had found in the grain store. He couldn't really grasp what the problem had been, but it had certainly upset his nurse when she found him at it. Neither was his mother terribly impressed when he tied together, end to end, a long string of freshly laundered bed linen that had been drying on the castle wall and fed that down the hole in the top of the well…

"Aubrey, did you hear me? Aubrey, come down, right now!" Nurse's voice pierced through Aubrey's preoccupation with the pain in his forearms and his disappointment at his unsuccessful attempt to catch a glimpse of the one thing of interest that he hoped he may have seen in the great expanse beyond his stone wall.

Realising he had been discovered, and secretly feeling a little relieved, Aubrey descended the remainder of the narrow stone steps, leaping from the fourth step to the ground, just to see how far he could go. Nurse finally reached the boy as he picked himself up from the dusty earth and, with her long, pale fingers cupping his shoulder, directed him back towards the confines of the house and to his lessons.

Today would not be the day his beloved father returned from his travels and tramped his weary horse up the final, wheel-rutted path to the gate of the lower keep. Nurse looked down on Aubrey's sweat-soaked head and, gently pushing sticky, dark curls from his forehead, spoke words of assurance that she knew he wanted to hear most of all in the world:

"He'll be home soon, child. He'll be home soon."

THE KING'S DINNER

Glistening silver plates and long-stemmed goblets…

Once upon a time, way, way, back, there was a huge hill in the middle of a wild, dense forest. This particular hill stood alone, rising above all the land around it. From its summit, anyone and everyone could be seen from miles and miles away. At the foot of its sweeping slopes was a river that bubbled over its stony bed with clear, sparkling water, and along the river's banks were sun-kissed fields that turned over easily to reveal rich, loamy soil - perfect for growing wheat, rye, and barley to grind into flour for baking bread. The surrounding wood was full of wild boar and deer. Huge birds of prey soared silently above the tops of its tallest trees in search of anything scuttling on the ground. Surely, this was the most perfect place to build a castle, and so, in time, inevitably, someone did just that.

Now, we know that only very rich and powerful, important people, can build themselves a castle, and the owner of this castle was just such a man. He was so important, he had a special title: 'The Earl of Oxford', and he looked after a man who was even more important than himself - the King of England!

One day, after the Earl had been working particularly hard looking after the King's business (you know: fighting battles, plundering villages, torturing traitors, that sort of thing), the King wanted to show him how grateful he was by honouring him in some way.

So, can you guess what the King wanted to do?

Would he give him a medal?

Ummmm….

Would he name something after him?

Errrmmmm…

What about a certificate, all written in fancy letters, to put up on his wall?

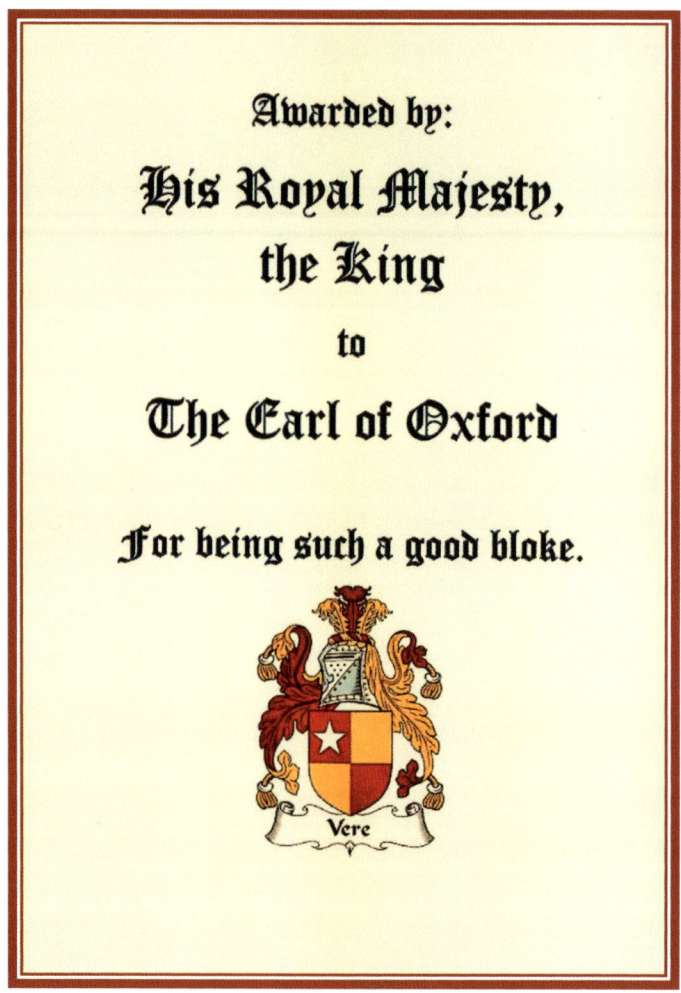

No, this King had different ideas about how to honour his nobles. The King decided to show his gratitude to the Earl by coming to his house for dinner.

Now, having a king at your house is quite an honour at any time, but way back then, it was something else altogether! The King called the Earl into his private chambers and told him of his intentions in person.

"I've decided," said the King,

"To do something

To show you that I am well pleased.

I've given it thought,

And think that I ought

Invite myself to yours for tea."

The colour drained from the Earl's face.

"T - t - t - tea?" he stammered.

"Sire, I am greatly honoured," he heard his mouth utter, as he bowed himself so low that his forehead nearly touched the ground.

All the while he was down there, his upside-down brain started to whirl and by the time he stood back up, he was in a complete and total flap.

"Oh, no!" said the Earl,

(But lest the King heard,

In his head) as he was dismissed...

Then panic set in;

With his head in a spin,

He started a big 'to do' list.

"Do we have enough food?

Are our fish any good?

Are there fowl on the lake and the river?

Should we hunt for some game?

Have the chickens all laid

Enough eggs to make the King's dinner?"

"And what if he stays…

For days and for days?

Can we get the bugs out of the beds?

And those tapestries hung?

Or clear out the dung

In the stables and rats from the shed?"

"Cook will go *INSANE!!*

She already complains

There's not enough help in the kitchen -

MORE buckets to fill

With old scraps of swill

For the pigs and plucking dead pigeons!"

"Scrub the steps,

Mop the floors,

Oil the hinges on the doors,

And polish the keys…and their locks.

I must empty the moat

And tether the goat,

And get that old woman out of the stocks!!"

And so the poor Earl, his head all in a tizz, rushed home to his castle where his wife, the Countess, was awaiting his return. He charged along the muddy village lanes, up the hill, over the drawbridge that crossed the rocky moat and through the castle gate. Leaping from his horse, he raced into the house, threw off his cloak and gloves, then rushed to find his wife and tell her the news.

Although having the King come to your house to dine with you was a very great honour, the reality of hosting the King was equally as challenging, because the King never arrived alone.

Now, I don't mean that he brought his wife, the Queen, or even had the kids tag along. When the King came to tea, so did a small army of officials and servants who came to see to all the King's needs. He had attendants for every occasion who accompanied him wherever he went. And because he was the King, he needed protection, so he also had a personal bodyguard with him at all times. And not just one bodyguard - he had a whole band of them. And, of course, there was his physician, in case he got sick, and a priest or two, in case he wanted to pray. And then there were all the porters who transported these very important members of the King's party and the baggage of these very important members of the King's party. Now times it by two, because the Queen had the same.

The King, the Queen, and all their royal attendants arrived by horse and cart, so even the horses needed looking after! The poor villagers who lived at the foot of the castle hill would have their lives turned upside down and there was never going to be enough food and drink for everyone – let alone places for them all to sleep. Was it any wonder the poor Earl was nearly having a fit by the time he arrived home to announce the intended visit to his wife?

The Earl of Oxford and his lady, the Countess, sat down together at their breakfast table to make preparations for the King's stay. The most pressing and urgent need was to make sure that the food they would be serving was just right. The King really loved his food, but the Queen had a delicate stomach, so she could be a bit picky.

Neither being an expert on food matters, the Earl and the Countess thought it wise to call upon the one person who was best placed to make sure the royal pair were well-fed and happy during their visit: the cook (who else?). So they summoned the cook for a family brainstorming session.

Cook duly took off her apron and hat, pushed her sweaty hair back from her forehead, and headed up from the depths of the steamy, airless kitchens to the posh part of the house. There, the Earl and the Countess were waiting for her with a pile of recipe books stacked in the centre of the large, scrubbed oak table.

"Oh, Cook!" they both yelped,

"We *SO* need your help!

We can't even offer pretence -

We've got books here by Beeton,

Jamie, Delia and Heston,

But they don't make a blind bit of sense!"

"These recipes sound great -
Like 'Tomato Stuffed Dates',
Okay, dates…but what's a tomato?
And nuts…in a roast?
Avocado on toast?
And what on earth is potato?"

"And all of these sweets
Made with sugar, as treats.
We've no sugar here, only honey!
The last thing we need
Is a disaster to feed
The King. That would *NOT* be funny!"

Well, the cook pursed her lips,
Put her hands on her hips
And declared, "Sir, Madam, I never!
You can't cook those things
To dine with the King,
'Cause that stuff's not yet been discovered."

"You'll have to make do

For a century or two,

Until some explorer goes and finds'em

And brings back them things

To impress some king

In the future…and *THEN* we can try'em."

"We'll start with some fish

Poached in cream, in a dish,

Some roe deer, a swan, and some ducklings.

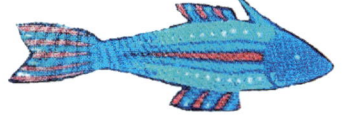

Then goose stuffed with doves,

A rabbit in cloves,

And a pig on a spit with good crackling."

"That's just for hor d'oeuvres -

Ten courses we'll serve -

More meat'n you'll poke with a stick.

And *LOADS* of game pies -

Such a feast for the eyes,

By the end, everyone'll be sick!"

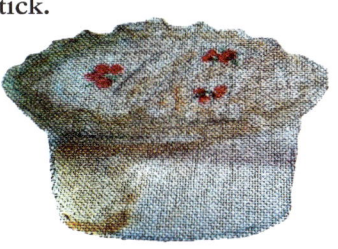

"Well," said the Earl to his wife, "it seems as though Cook has everything in hand. Sounds like she knows just what to do."

"Thank goodness," replied the Countess. "I wonder how these recipe books came to be in our cupboard. I'm glad I won't be expected to eat potatoes or tomatoes. After all, they might be the sort of thing only peasants eat. Heaven forbid if they had got hold of them down in the village, they might start sticking them in their allotments. I'm not even sure they are not poisonous!"

So the Earl went about the business of preparing his castle home for the King's imminent arrival. The poor villagers started secretly hiding anything and everything they had in their thatch and mud cottages in the hope that something would survive the impending invasion. Since everything was owned by their lord, the Earl, including themselves, they had to be especially careful not to be caught. Even the nuns in their cloister started squirreling away anything of value, safe from the prying eyes (and thieving fingers) of any of the rougher sort of hanger-on who may be tagging along behind the King's retinue.

But the Earl was preoccupied with his own preparations. Everything in the castle on the top of the hill had to be spotlessly clean and tidy. The Earl did not want anything to spoil his royal master's special visit. He really, really, really wanted to impress him.

Finally, the momentous day dawned and the King arrived for dinner. The banqueting hall in the great keep was decked out gaily in magnificent colours. Tapestries hung from the walls and silken banners draped like floral garlands from the high gallery. Glistening silver plates and long-stemmed goblets were laid out in perfect formation on the top table where the King and Queen would be seated. On each side would be the Earl and the

Countess, then, going outward, the most important nobles, according to their rank, and the most eminent bishops of the Church. All the guests chatted away merrily as they waited for Their Majesties' arrival to be announced. A great hush descended as the royal pair progressed into the room and were escorted to their seats. Everyone else could now follow. Finally, with everything and everyone in their proper places, dinner service was commenced.

One by one, the gleaming silver dishes of the first course were brought up from the kitchens, steam escaping from the wonderful delicacies laid out neatly beneath their domed covers. The air was filled with the aroma of roasted meats and crisp pastry pies. There was wine and ale aplenty, ready to fill the goblets of every diner. Everything was just perfect!

Cook had done a fantastic job down in her stuffy, hot kitchen. Her food (enough to feed an army) not only smelled amazing but it was also decorated beautifully with herbs and flowers, berries and spices. All sorts of elaborate patterns were baked into the tops of the pies, showing what sort of filling each one contained.

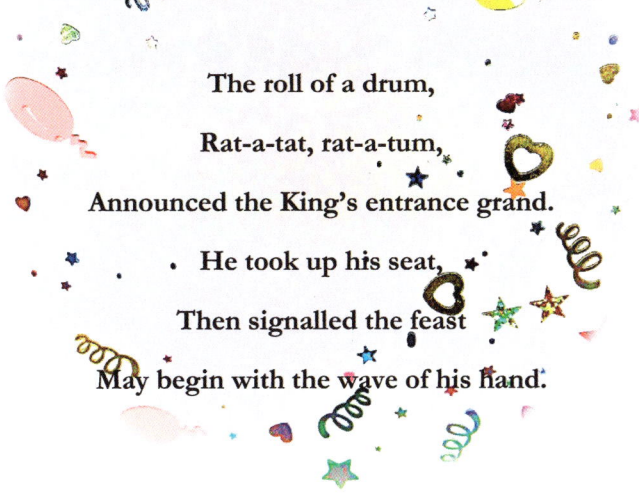

The roll of a drum,

Rat-a-tat, rat-a-tum,

Announced the King's entrance grand.

He took up his seat,

Then signalled the feast

May begin with the wave of his hand.

With platters held high,

The servants came nigh

And ceremoniously lifted the covers,

Revealing delights

For taste, smell and sight,

And looked to the King for approval.

        The King then surveyed

        All that was laid

        Before him and sniffed it quite loudly.

        While the Queen gave a grin,

        He rubbed his great chin,

        And Cook stood by the door proudly.

He hummed for a while -

With a hint of a smile -

Then leaned back in his seat and spoke:

"My, this looks swell,

And smells good as well,

But I fancy a *BIG MAC* and a *COKE!*"

And now the true story…

In medieval times, roads were often no more than tracks made by the wheels of peasants' carts: muddy, churned up by animal hooves, and often, almost impassable. It was difficult to keep in touch with other people who lived further away than a person could reasonably walk. Most ordinary folk were born, lived and died in the same village, as the lord of the estate owned not only the land, but many of the villagers who lived and worked on it.

These workers were called 'serfs' and lived in close proximity to the protection of the lord's seat or main home, from where he administered his estates. First they worked his land and brought their produce up to the walled enclosure that surrounded his home to service the needs of the residents of the castle. They were permitted small parcels of land on which they could then produce food for their own households. In exchange for their labour and lack of personal freedom, they looked to their lord for protection in times of conflict. Assuming they were not able-bodied men who might be useful in battle, they would be permitted to seek refuge within the walls of the bailey should their village come under attack.

Poaching (hunting or fishing on land that belonged to the lord) had been illegal from Saxon times, and the Normans also enforced these laws. Punishment could range from fines to the death penalty, which was the fate of anyone caught hunting deer in the royal forests.

In Norman times, kings and queens would travel about the kingdom, staying at the largest houses of their favoured courtiers. They had what was called an 'itinerant court' and it was a great privilege to host the king and his party of attendants who could stay for a week or more. Their hosts would provide hunting and feasting by way of entertainment, but there were also political and judicial matters to attend to.

On the king's part, there were great advantages to travelling in this way around the kingdom, for the hosts with whom he stayed had to provide for his entire household and servants from their own funds. This made it quite economical for the king to keep going from house to house, although his courtiers were known to bankrupt themselves in their efforts to impress their sovereign.

Such tours would be undertaken in the summer months. This was an added advantage for the king's household, as the residence he was temporarily vacating could be thoroughly stripped bare and cleaned out in his absence. Since straw was laid down on the floors which became home to fleas and such-like, this was a very welcome opportunity. Also, the worst of the summer stench from the unsanitary conditions of London could be avoided. There was no form of public sanitation in London until many centuries later. All sorts of refuse, including the rotting entrails from the butchers' shops, would be dumped into the Thames.

THE TALE OF TWO MATILDAS

The Empress Matilda and Geoffrey of Anjou

This is the story of a very powerful family who caused the people of England a great deal of trouble and sorrow, long ago, in a time that we now call 'the Anarchy'. Before we begin, let's look quickly at the word 'anarchy'.

'Anarchy' means to be without rule or order. It is made up of the word 'arch', which comes from the Greek language of ancient times, meaning 'rule', with the prefix 'an', which means 'not', or 'without'. And so 'the Anarchy' is the name given to the time between 1135 and 1153 when the whole realm was at war with one another. When the people of the same country fight each other, we call it a 'civil war'.

So, how did this sorry situation come about?

When William the Conqueror defeated King Harold and took the English throne from him, he became the head of a new family of rulers called the 'House of Normandy'. William had fought hard to bring the English people under his control. However, the problem with fighting to get what you want all your life is that you can't control what will happen to it after you die. So it was for William and his descendants. Things went well, until William's last surviving son, Henry I, died, leaving only a daughter to inherit the throne. Before he died, Henry had made all his nobles swear an oath that they would accept his daughter, Matilda, as their queen. However, Henry's nephew, Stephen, wanted what King Henry had left behind (the throne of England) for himself, and although he swore he would support Matilda, when the crunch came, he changed his mind.

In those days, nobody really wanted a woman as their ruler. They thought women were weak and rulers had to be quite tough, as they always seemed to be fighting wars. Strong rulers had to put on armour, mount their horses, and lead their troops into battle. They had to be able to wield enormous, heavy swords and be ready to hack their opponents to death with them. Hardly appropriate work for the soft, white petal hands of the delicate creatures considered to be 'the fairer sex'. But they were very much mistaken about Matilda! She may not have been physically battle-ready, but she was a fearless and determined woman who was willing to fight hard politically for what she believed was rightly hers. Unfortunately, she also was thought to be quite proud and haughty (which means she thought she was better than everybody else).

Now, William the Conqueror had also had a daughter who had married a Norman nobleman and gone to live in France. She was Stephen's mother, and because his father died when Stephen was young, Stephen was sent to be brought up by his uncle, King Henry, in England. So Stephen was William the Conqueror's grandson and since Stephen's mother and King Henry were brother and sister, Stephen and Matilda were cousins, just a few years apart in age.

Most of us know our cousins well, and Stephen grew up with Matilda in her mother's court. However, Matilda was sent to live in Germany when she was only eight years old because she was going to marry the German King, who was also the Emperor of the Holy Roman Empire. After her marriage, Matilda became Empress Matilda.

Just to add a bit more confusion, Stephen had a wife who was also called Matilda. Stephen's Matilda and Empress Matilda were also cousins, but this time through their mothers' family. The two Matildas' mothers were sisters, daughters of Margaret, Queen of Scotland. The Empress's mother (also called Matilda) was Stephen's Matilda's godmother as well as her aunt. I guess they didn't mind sharing names or have any idea (or maybe care?) how much confusion it would cause schoolchildren many centuries later.

The name 'Matilda' was often shortened to 'Maude', so to help follow their story, we are going to refer to the Empress as 'Maude' and Stephen's wife as 'Matilda'.

Maude was quite a character. Married as a young teenager, she travelled to Rome where she was fully involved in the business of being an Empress. Sadly, her husband died and Maude returned to her father, who promptly organised another husband for her.

Maude was less than impressed with her father's choice - Geoffrey of Anjou. He was only a child of 13 (she was 25) and a mere Count as well! She refused to marry him. Although she was a widow and an Empress, Henry locked her in her room until she gave in and agreed to marry Count Geoffrey. After they married, she ran back home to her father again. Eventually, she returned to Geoffrey, but she kept her much more important title of 'Empress Maude'.

What was our other Matilda up to while her cousin was busy being an Empress? Our second Matilda became the wife of Maude's cousin from the other side of the family, Stephen. It was this Matilda who would become the Queen of England when her husband, Stephen, was crowned the King.

So, what was all the fighting about?

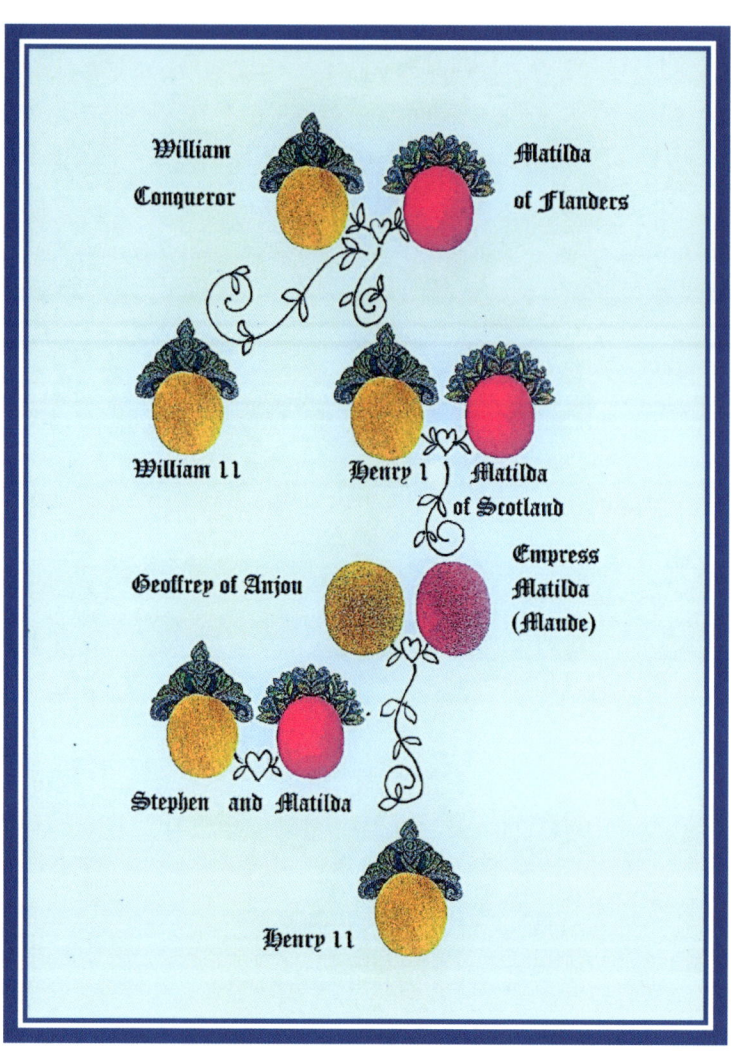

The crowned descendants of William the Conquerer

Well, all three cousins were in France when the news arrived that King Henry had died. His daughter and nominated successor, Empress Maude, was with her husband, Count Geoffrey, in Anjou (which is inland) fighting some of his battles with him. Stephen and Matilda, however, were in Boulogne, right on the coast, so Stephen jumped into a ship and raced to London.

His wife, Matilda, stopped just long enough to deliver her baby and then followed right behind. There, the bishops and noblemen of the city crowned Stephen as king, despite the promise they had all made to Henry (including Stephen) that the crown would go to Empress Maude.

Maude, in the meantime, was busy fighting her husband's battles in France alongside her half-brother, Robert. Robert was furious at Stephen's trickery, and after a few years, he persuaded Maude to return to England to claim her crown.

The Church supported King Stephen because his brother was an important bishop and the Empress Maude had the support of her Uncle David, who also happened to be the King of Scotland. It seemed all the relatives got involved! Then, if they had a falling out with each other, they simply switched sides. And then switched back again! And so began nearly two decades of warfare in England which would finally end in a stalemate, neither side being able to gain complete control of power.

Kings and queens were not the only people willing to switch sides if they thought it would be to their advantage. Being flexible when it came to allegiances could be the best course of action for noblemen to attain wealth and social standing, although it could be a risky business.

The de Veres held the hereditary title of Lord Great Chamberlain: a very prestigious and responsible position in the royal household. The role of Lord Great Chamberlain included receiving and paying out moneys owed to the King and he also had access to the royal bed chamber, which was the place where the sovereign's person was most vulnerable.

Aubrey de Vere II held the position of Lord Great Chamberlain in King Stephen's household but was murdered in a riot in London during the time when Stephen had been captured and imprisoned in Lincoln Castle. His successor, Aubrey III, thought he'd better change his family's allegiance, so he courted the Empress Maude, instead. She offered him, and he accepted, the title of 'Earl of Oxenford', later shortened to 'Oxford'. That proved to be a bit embarrassing when King Stephen was released in exchange for Maud's brother Robert and had himself crowned again. The Earl quickly changed sides again.

But back to our story…

First, early on in their struggles, Stephen captured Maude, but for some reason or other, let her go again. Later on, as mentioned above, Maude's troops captured Stephen and put him in prison in Lincoln Castle. Maude raced straight to London to be crowned queen, but an angry London mob chased her out of the Palace of Westminster while she was having her tea and she had to run for her life!

Along the way back to safe territory in the southwest, she became trapped in Oxford Castle, which had been surrounded by Stephen's men. Clever and daring as she was, she crept out of a castle gate with a few of her men in the dead of night. She was supposedly dressed all in white, so she wouldn't be seen escaping through the snow.

Then, as mentioned, Maude's brother, Robert, was captured by Queen Matilda, who was carrying on the fight while Stephen was in prison. Being very practical about it, Maude and Matilda simply exchanged the two prisoners and carried on fighting. Stephen went back to London and had himself crowned as king again…just to be sure.

If only our first Earl of Oxford had had a crystal ball with which to see the future! He now had to make peace with Stephen again, (which he promptly did) although shortly after, he was arrested, thrown into prison, then forced to surrender his castle at Hedingham in order to regain his liberty. He can't have stayed in Stephen's bad books for long, though, for he was later to return to his castle at Hedingham and marry Euphemia, a close friend of Queen Matilda.

It is never a good thing when people go to war against each other. It's usually the poor and the helpless bystanders who suffer the most. Spies on both sides were going about, seeing who was doing or saying things. There was no longer law and order in the land. Gangs of bandits and robbers terrified people as they tried to go about their daily business - often they were gangs of soldiers, whom everyone feared. It must have been a frightening time in which to live, particularly as the poorest of ordinary folk, called 'serfs', belonged to their lord and could not leave his land without his permission.

Eventually, Maude had control over the southwest of England and Stephen over the southeast. While all this was going on, the land-owning barons of Scotland, Wales, and the north of England were becoming dangerously powerful. The kingdom was in danger of coming under attack from without, as well as within!

Eventually, Empress Maude returned to Normandy, and her son, Henry, continued the fight. Back and forth, back and forth it went until finally, they all lost their taste (and ran out of enough money) for fighting and began to talk instead. They decided that Henry would rule after Stephen's death instead of Stephen's own children. Maude continued to look after Henry's interests in Normandy when he eventually ruled in England. She lived a long life and was a very powerful woman and well-respected political advisor. Maude died at the grand old age (in those days) of 67 and was buried in France.

And what of Matilda and Stephen? King Stephen and Queen Matilda had a strong marriage and were devoted to one another. Stephen had an easy-going, likeable personality, which, at times, had allowed others the opportunity to challenge his rule. He and Matilda left a different type of legacy from that of Maude.

Matilda had been a brave warrior on her husband's behalf. She was also a calm and skillful negotiator. However, Matilda was not so much interested in politics and power as she was in doing good things for people. Queen Matilda was a devout woman (which means she was concerned about spiritual things) who founded nunneries and monasteries. She supported the work of the Knights Templar: a religious order who fought in the Crusades and founded their estate at Cressing Temple. She died of a fever at Hedingham Castle in 1152, while visiting her good friend, Euphemia, Countess of Oxford. It was at Faversham Abbey, which she and Stephen had founded, that Queen Matilda was finally buried. Stephen died shortly after and was buried alongside Matilda. Maud's son, Henry, (Henry I's grandson) was crowned Henry II of England in 1154.

THE SIEGE OF HEDINGHAM CASTLE

The moon hung white and low…

The sky was black.

The air was still.

The moon hung white and low.

A castle stood tall,

On top of a hill

In the soft moonlight aglow.

The pale stone face

Of its menacing keep

Leered over the castle wall -

A fortress, thrust

Into the sky,

Defying one and all.

Now, King John

Needed more money.

He'd spent all his on wars!

It's not a small thing

To be a great king,

But he'd taxed his subjects poor.

"More money! More money!

MORE MONEY!!! "

It never seemed to end,

'Til their cupboards were bare,

And his noblemen dared

To force the King's will to bend.

The Earl of Oxford cried,

"NO!!!!!

There is no more money to spare!

I'm going home

To Hedingham

'Cause you're just not being fair!"

Well, that was just

Asking for trouble!

What mischief would now unfurl?

Whatever now

Would King John do

To such a churlish earl?

The King's eyes grew wide,

Then *POPPED!*

Steam blew from the royal ears.

His beard trembled,

His jaw dropped,

And his eyes filled up with tears.

"Get my horse! Get my troops!

Get my armour!

Get my standard, my shield,

GET! MY! SWORD!!!

I'll teach that upstart baron

To speak back to his lord!"

And so the siege

Of Hedingham

Began that very night.

The King's troops

In clanking armour

Rolled up for a darn good fight.

GET! MY! SWORD!!!

Within the same hour,

The Earl raced to his tower,

And blocked off all of the doors.

"We've nothing to fear,

If we just stay in here,"

He promised his men, all assured.

"Come out and fight,

You excuse for a knight!

Come out," yelled King John, "before

We climb to the top

Of this puny hill

And tear down your pitiful walls!"

Now old Oxford was shrewd.

He'd expected a feud,

So he had a few tricks in his box.

He'd stocked up his tower

With archers and arrows,

And big heaps of dirty, old rocks.

The air was crisp and clear.
The moon rose round and bright.
The crackling campfires of the King
Shot sparks into the night.

Then with the first ray

Of the new day,

Up went John's rallying shout -

"Get up that hill!

Get over that wall!

We'll burn the whole lot of them out!"

With raised sword and shield,

And crunching of steel,

Upwards they heaved and clawed.

But the Earl in his tower

Sent them off with a shower

Of arrows and rocks, large and small.

From morning 'til night,

The King's men would fight

To conquer it once and for all.

But each night the lights

From the tower's great heights

Winked smugly back over the wall.

"What shall we do, Sire?

We can't take this tower.

They just laugh from the top of their keep!"

"There's just one thing left,

That I can suggest -

We must starve them out, I think."

"We could block off the gate,

Surround them and wait -

Our men hiding right round the wall.

Their food will run low

And before they know,

They'll have to surrender it all."

Well, the King didn't know

About the fishpond below,

Where the Earl's men could slip out and crawl

With a net and a sack

To bring some fish back

And sneak into the tower with their haul.

They just laugh from the top of their keep

So with no end in sight,

John squared up to fight

And sent his troops back up to brawl.

"Give it all that you've got!

We'll *MAKE* them come out!"

And once more they assaulted the wall.

The Earl's men chucked sticks,

And stones, and bricks,

Down from their tower so tall,

And his archers drew bows,

And shot arrows below,

From the thin slits in the keep's walls.

But still the troops came,

Again and again,

To batter the tower: *WHAM! WHAM!*

And they swarmed all around

The stairs on the ground,

To smash down the door with their rams.

THERE'S A LOAD OF OLD FISH IN THIS POT!

Well, it wasn't long

Before the rocks were all gone,

And the archers had emptied their quivers,

So they boiled up some oil,

And poured *THAT* down the wall -

And anything else they could deliver.

With the tower now bare,

(In some despair)

The Earl cried, "What else have we got?"

And a young boy yelled up

From the kitchens below…

"THERE'S A LOAD OF OLD FISH IN THIS POT!"

Now old fish stink like…

Stinky old fish,

And the stinkier they are, the better.

The old Earl grinned

And rubbed his chin.

"Let's teach the King's men a lesson!"

From the top of the roof, the rotting fish flew

From the top of the roof

The rotting fish flew.

SPLAT! SPLOSH! Those stink bombs whopped them.

And stinky old fish guts

Exploded all over

Their helmets and stank up their armour.

So how did it end -

This battle between

King John and his wayward equerry?

Well, both are long gone,

But their lesson lives on -

Sometimes it's just best to say, "Sorry."

The spring air is warm,

The sun is on high,

And daffodils sway in the breeze.

And the lofty, white walls

Of a tower so tall

Rise boldly above the great trees.

And now the true story...

King John was an unpopular king who ruled England from 1199 until his death in 1216. The last of five sons of Henry II, he was not expected to reign. His policies of heavy taxation and his abuse of power led to his English nobles forcing him to agree to terms of conduct which were laid out in a document called 'Magna Carta' or 'Great Charter'. He came from his hunting lodge at Odiham Castle in Hampshire to meet with his rebellious barons in a field beside the Thames at Runnymede, near Staines.

John, true to his nature, did not honour the terms to which he had agreed and this set off a period of rebellion against him, called 'The Baron Wars'. The Earl of Oxford was one of the twenty-five nobles who had been charged with ensuring that the King adhered to the terms of the Magna Carta. As a result of John's refusal to do so, the Earl of Oxford took up arms against John and joined with other rebel barons to offer the crown of England to Prince Louis of France. In 1215, the King's forces laid siege to the Earl of Oxford's castle at Hedingham, although John was not personally present.

King John's men were confident that they could force a surrender by cutting off food supplies to the castle, however, Oxford and his men had both a water supply and access to the castle's fish ponds. They are recorded as having taunted the King's men by throwing fish at them over the castle wall.

The castle was eventually surrendered. It was held briefly by King John, but recaptured and returned to the Earl of Oxford, whose direct descendants retained it until the earldom expired with the death of the 20th Earl of Oxford in 1703.

THE EARL'S NEW SHOES

He does like to think he looks handsome

The Earl is having a party!

He's decided to have some fun

In his spanking new castle

At Hedingham,

Because the 'doing up'

Has all been done!

It has a shiny new gate,

And a bridge, good and straight,

Right over the freshly cleaned moat.

Plus a nice, new brick house,

And an *ENORMOUS* square tower

With a banqueting hall to boot!

His wife does a twirl

Around the room with the Earl,

For she simply *LOVES* to entertain!

But then, standing before

Her big wardrobe doors,

Her enthusiasm soon starts to wane…

"My dear," she utters,

(As the Earl's heart flutters...

He sort of knows what's coming next)

"I've nothing to wear!

My clothes and my hair

Are not quite as our friends will expect."

"I can't wear these old rags,

And this old handbag!

You know that our guests will all be

Dressed up to the nines

In clothing so fine.

I need a new dress and accessories."

Well the Earl knows the game

They all have to play

(And he does like to think he looks handsome).

"But the trouble," he thought,

"To keep up at court,

Is it costs you a proper king's ransom!"

I can't wear these old rags and this old handbag!

"Shall we make it a day?

We'll book in and pay

That guy who does royal robes and tights,

And see what he can do

In time for us two

To get 'Best Dressed in Ball' on the night."

So off the pair fly

Up to London to spy

Out what new things have come from abroad.

They try them all on

And parade themselves round

The tailor's shop on the King's Road.

"This ye-ar," sniffs the tailor,

"The shoooulders are broader

And the waists are vurry, vurry tight.

And the length of the shooooe

Must be at least twooooo

Times the foot, if they are to look rrrrright."

So the Earl takes a chair,

And tries on a pair,

Then saunters (as you do…) round the place.

But the toes start to bend,

And so in the end,

He trips and falls flat on his face!

While the Earl's on the floor,

Wifey comes through the door

Of the changing room in a new frock,

With a hat that's *SO* big,

She can't see a thing,

Trips over him and lands with a shock!

With legs in the air,

And very squiffy hair,

She rolls round the floor in her skirts.

While her husband's now shouting,

She sits up and starts pouting,

For her pride is considerably hurt.

But one must just do

What one just must do,

So they purchase dress, hat, shoes and all.

The Earl has a few days

To figure out ways

NOT to land on his face at the ball.

First, he tries, in his room,

To master one shoe,

Lifting his foot up high, then flicking

His toe in the air,

And, while holding a chair,

Stamps his heel down before the toe trips him.

"This is not a good look,"

He decides, "It took

So much effort to walk in these slippers

That I looked quite absurd,

And walked like a bird -

A penguin…with a big pair of flippers."

Well the Earl didn't get

To be a big-shot

By accepting defeat - giving in,

So a new pair of shoes

Was not going to undo

What a lifetime of war had taught him.

With so much at stake,

The Earl struggles to break-in

His shoes and learn to walk right.

He rolls to the sides,

Shoves some padding inside,

Even thinks about sitting all night.

The big day soon dawns,

But still he's not learned,

And wouldn't, even if he'd had years!

So, at the end of his rope,

His only hope

Is to ask his wife for ideas.

Even thinks about sitting all night

Now, the Countess is done

Putting her hair in a bun

Pinned under her new hat (called a wimple).

With her skirts now just right,

And her bodice pulled tight,

She looks around for something simple.

And then it just came!

A solution so plain

It would solve his dilemma with ease.

She ties the end of some ribbon

To the toe of each slipper,

And the other end up round his knees.

And off they both flounce

To their tower to dance

In the banqueting hall with their friends,

And they're such a success

With their new mode of dress,

That they start a new fashion trend!

HURRAY! for the Earl!

HURRAY! for his wife!

And for those who love clothes with a passion!

For what would we do

Without silly shoes

To make us all martyrs to fashion?

And now the true story...

Clothing in medieval times was made of natural fibres, like wool and linen. Cloth could be left undyed - grey, brown, or cream, depending on the colour of the fibres from which it had been woven. However, vegetable and mineral dyes were well known and could be used to produce a range of colours that ordinary people could afford. The most luxurious fabrics, such as silk, were imported to England from Europe and the Middle East.

Particular colours of cloth were used to indicate social status, and, for a long time, it was illegal for someone of a lower class to wear cloth dyed certain colours. For example, the colour purple (ranging from reds to blues) could not, from ancient times, be worn by anyone other than royalty.

Some other aspects of clothing were subject to rules and regulations as well. Only the nobility could wear fur trims, for example. Women of the lower classes were not permitted to have silver detail on their girdles (which were like belts). For those who were permitted, and could afford such luxury, wearing fantastically elaborate clothing was a statement of wealth and status. Such things as cloth woven with gold thread, and rare and expensive silks, became forbidden imports. This was partly due to the concern that English money should not be spent abroad, importing cloth, but also to maintain a clear distinction between the classes of people that made up English society.

Some of the fashions were extreme, such as the pointy-toed shoes called 'poulaines' that feature in our poem and men seemed to love fashion as much as women. However, wealthy ladies could enjoy wearing amazingly fashioned head coverings. They would totter around balancing elaborate constructions (called 'wimples') on their heads. These hats were made of embroidered cloth with fine linen or silk veils flowing from their peaks.

Castle Hedingham Today

The Essex village of Castle Hedingham is still dominated by Hedingham Castle, the remains of the original castle built by the Norman invaders, the de Veres. The 'chocolate box' village with its rows of crooked cottages, twisted lanes, and abundance of wisteria and hollyhocks nestles quaintly around the base of the castle's promontory.

Ancestral home to the Earls of Oxford, all that remains of the castle's oldest phase of building is its square, stone keep. A Tudor-period arched bridge of red brick connects the upper bailey to the lower bailey, where an imposing Palladian-style house presently sits.

In the village below, St Nicholas's Church still provides a home to a vibrant Christian community and serves the interests of many of the residents of the village. The Benedictine nunnery has long gone, having been granted back to the Earl of Oxford during the time of the dissolution of the monastries under Henry VIII. Along with it went any evidence of its rumoured secret tunnel. There is also no visible trace of the hospital which had been founded near the entrance to the castle grounds.

Although the direct line of the de Vere family died out with the 20th Earl of Oxford in 1703, visitors to the surrounding towns and villages in Essex and Suffolk may find reminders of the de Vere family's influence – from the star design built into the tower of St Andrews church, Earls Colne, to the Blue Boar public houses named after the family's blue boar crest. The castle, which is in private ownership, and the village community, host many events throughout the year which may be enjoyed by locals and visitors alike.

Carol Sullivan Johnson lives in Halstead, Essex, with her husband, Harvey, and works as a private tutor. She has written and illustrated a biography entitled 'Yards and Fences, Gates and Roads' about growing up in Brisbane, Australia in the 1960s, and also 'A Tale of Two Mice', a morality tale in verse. Both books were written for children.

Her other books include 'God's Plan, God's Power', a seven-module study program on Christian faith and practice, and 'A Little Book about God's Great Love'.

Printed by Amazon Italia Logistica S.r.l.
Torrazza Piemonte (TO), Italy